sundance
publishing

LITTLE RED
READERS

Making a Cake

PETER SLOAN &
SHERYL SLOAN

Dad is making a cake.
It is a carrot cake.
My brother and I
want to help him.

My brother mixes the butter
with the sugar in a bowl.
Now it looks smooth.

I put in two eggs.
Some eggshells fall
into the bowl.
I lift the shell out
with a spoon.

4

Now my brother adds
the flour and grated carrot.
Then he pours in some milk.
He mixes everything
together quickly.
Dad has the cake pan
ready.

The oven is already hot.
I spoon the batter
into the pan.
Dad puts the pan
in the oven.

6

My brother and I
lick the spoons.
This is the best part
of helping Dad make
a cake!

When the cake is baked
and iced, we eat it.